IS-130: Exercise Evaluation and Improvement Planning

By

Fema

1/23/2008

IS-130 - Exercise Evaluation and Improvement Planning

Lesson 1: Exercise Evaluation Overview

Exercise Evaluation and Improvement Planning

The purpose of this course is to provide learners with an understanding of the need for exercise evaluation and improvement planning, and to equip learners with methodologies for both.

This online course will:

- Provide the base for evaluation of exercises in which Federal, State, territorial, tribal, and local jurisdictions participate along with non-governmental and private sector organizations.
- Reinforce identified training standards.
- Provide for evaluation of readiness.
- Support the National Preparedness Goal and National Incident Management System (NIMS).
- Provide structure, multi-year planning, tools, and guidance necessary for individuals to build and sustain exercise programs that enhance public and private sector preparedness.

Course Objectives

The focus of this course is on the evaluation and improvement planning process. Its purpose is to support the individual who manages, participates in, reviews, or sponsors the exercise evaluation or improvement planning function.

At the end of the Exercise Evaluation and Improvement Planning course, participants will be able to:

- Describe the need for a systematic approach to exercise evaluation.
- List the eight steps of the exercise evaluation and improvement planning process.
- Identify pre-exercise activities necessary for a successful evaluation.
- Explain the function of Exercise Evaluation Guides (EEGs) and their relationship to the Target Capabilities List (TCL)/Universal Task List (UTL).
- Describe post-exercise analysis activities.

- Explain the purpose and format of the After-Action Report/Improvement Plan (AAR/IP).
- Describe how the Corrective Action Program (CAP) translates exercise outcomes into continual improvements to preparedness.

Estimated Time to Course Completion: 5 hours

Course Organization

This course consists of eight lessons:

- Lesson 1: Exercise Evaluation Overview
- Lesson 2: Exercise Evaluation Process
- Lesson 3: Planning and Organizing the Evaluation
- Lesson 4: Observing the Exercise and Collecting Data
- Lesson 5: Analyzing Data
- Lesson 6: The After-Action Report and After-Action Conference
- Lesson 7: The Corrective Action Program
- Lesson 8: Lesson Summary

It is designed for people who will manage the exercise evaluation and improvement planning function within their jurisdiction. Several lessons address specific evaluation functions and techniques, and could be used in evaluator training prior to an exercise. However, this course primarily focuses on planning, staffing, organizing, directing, and coordinating the exercise evaluation and improvement planning function.

Course Background

This course was introduced by the Federal Emergency Management Agency (FEMA) in 1992 as an instructor-led course. In 2002, the Department of Homeland Security (DHS) developed the Homeland Security Exercise and Evaluation Program (HSEEP), policy and guidance for designing, developing, conducting, and evaluating exercises.

DHS and FEMA have worked collectively and collaboratively to standardize the language and concepts used in the exercise evaluation process. As such, this course has been reissued, incorporating the terms and methods outlined in HSEEP.

Course Prerequisites

Before completing this course, you should have already completed the following course:

- IS-120.a: Introduction to Exercises

This course is also available as a paper-based independent study course.

Lesson Overview

This lesson provides an overview of the exercise development, evaluation, and improvement planning process. It also previews what you will learn in other course lessons about the exercise evaluation and improvement planning process.

Lesson Objectives

After completing this lesson, you will be able to:

- Define exercise evaluation and improvement planning.
- Describe why systematic evaluation and improvement planning is important.

What is an Exercise?

As you learned in IS-120.b: Introduction to Exercises, an exercise is a focused practice activity that places players in a simulated situation. During the situation, players need to function in the capacity that would be expected of them in a real event.

As you will learn throughout this course, exercises are conducted to support an overall assessment of a given capability.

There are two main benefits of conducting exercises:

- **Individual and team training:** Exercising enables people to practice and gain experience in their roles.
- **System improvement:** Exercising improves an organization's system for managing emergencies.

These benefits come not just from exercising, but from planning the exercise, controlling the exercise, evaluating the exercise, and acting upon resulting recommendations. An exercise has value only when it leads to improvement.

Exercise Evaluation Defined

Evaluation can be defined as the act of reviewing or observing and recording exercise activity or conduct, assessing behaviors or activities against exercise objectives, and noting strengths, weaknesses, deficiencies, or other observations.

Evaluation should not be a single event in the exercise process; instead, it should be carefully integrated into overall exercise design.

The output of exercise evaluation is information used to improve performance. For this reason, exercise evaluation is part of an on-going process of improvements to preparedness.

Click on this link to review the Homeland Security Exercise and Evaluation Program (HSEEP) Policy and Guidance, Volume III, which contains detailed information on exercise evaluation.

Why Exercise Evaluation and Improvement Planning is Important

Since September 11, 2001, Federal, State, and local governments have made major investments in improving the nation's preparedness to prevent, respond to, and recover from major disasters. The best way to determine the impact of these investments is to conduct preparedness exercises.

When conducted systematically, these exercises serve as gap analysis tools, helping communities identify gaps in policy, training and equipment. In this way, systematic exercises lay the foundation for a continuous cycle of improvement planning. They therefore maximize the value of preparedness investments to the community.

Lesson 2: Exercise Evaluation Process

Lesson Overview

This lesson introduces the Homeland Security Exercise and Evaluation Program (HSEEP) developed by the Department of Homeland Security (DHS).

Lesson Objectives

Upon completing this lesson, you will be able to:

- Describe the eight steps of the HSEEP evaluation and improvement planning process.
- Explain the relationship between the HSEEP process and a Corrective Action Program (CAP).
- Identify key tools to use within the evaluation and improvement planning process.

Applying Methodologies

The purpose of the Homeland Security Exercise and Evaluation Program (HSEEP) is to provide a national standard for exercises. This standard is based on capabilities-based planning and emphasizes the need to build capabilities suitable for responding to a wide range of hazards.

HSEEP provides consistent terminology and tools for all exercise planners. Although these features are standardized, HSEEP can be applied to the full spectrum of hazardous scenarios and incidents.

The HSEEP process has eight steps:

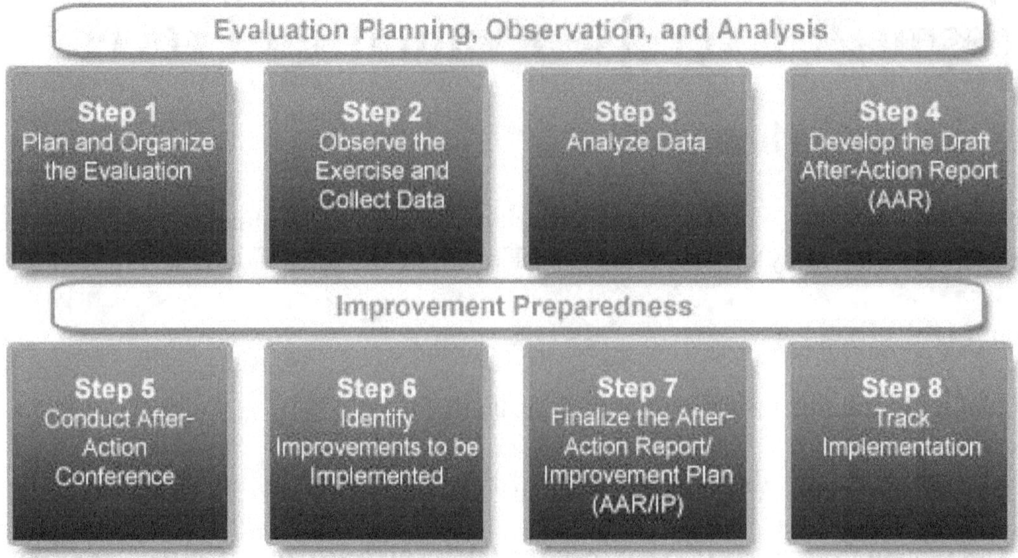

Evaluation and Improvement Process: Steps 1-4

The first four steps of the process address evaluation planning, observation, and analysis.

1. **Plan and Organize the Evaluation.** Step 1 is part of the exercise design process. In it, the Exercise Planning Team determines what information to collect, who will collect it, and how it will be collected.
2. **Observe the Exercise and Collect Data.** Step 2 occurs during the exercise. In it, expert evaluators collect data and record observations. They also collect data from records and logs.
3. **Analyze Data.** During Step 3, evaluators use Exercise Evaluation Guides (EEGs) to analyze data and reconstruct exercise events.
4. **Develop the Draft After-Action Report.** In Step 4, the Evaluation Team develops the draft After-Action Report (AAR). It describes what happened in the exercise, issues to be addressed, best practices, and recommendations for improvement.

Evaluation and Improvement Process: Steps 5-8

The second four steps of the process are detailed below. These steps focus on using information gained from exercises to implement improvements to a jurisdiction's capabilities.

5. **Conduct an After-Action Conference.** In Step 5, evaluators, participating agency representatives, and senior officials attend an After-Action Conference. Its

purpose is to review the draft After-Action Report (AAR), define actions agencies can take to improve performance, and validate recommendations.

6. **Identify Improvements to be Implemented.** During the After-Action Conference, attendees identify corrective actions that address the areas for improvement and recommendations listed in the draft AAR. These corrective actions are captured on the Improvement Plan (IP).
7. **Finalize the After-Action Report/Improvement Plan (AAR/IP).** In Step 7, the exercise planning and evaluation teams incorporate corrections, clarifications, and other participant feedback into the AAR/IP.
8. **Track Implementation.** In Step 8, each agency or jurisdiction monitors corrective actions identified in the finalized AAR/IP.

HSEEP and the Corrective Action Program (CAP)

The jurisdiction's work is not done when it has completed these eight steps. Long after the exercise is over, the jurisdiction's program managers will track and analyze the implementation of corrective actions listed in the After-Action Report/Improvement Plan (AAR/IP).

By tracking and recording progress on corrective actions, the jurisdiction engages in a continuous Corrective Action Program (CAP). Through the CAP, the implementation of corrective actions leads to concrete improvements to preparedness.

HSEEP Tools and Resources

The Homeland Security Exercise and Evaluation Program (HSEEP) offers tools and resources to support exercise planners throughout the eight-step process.

These tools include:

- **Exercise Evaluation Guides (EEGs).** EEGs provide evaluators with consistent standards and guidelines for observation, data collection, analysis, and report writing.
- **After-Action Report/Improvement Plan (AAR/IP) Template.** A standard template is available for the AAR/IP, the main product of the evaluation and improvement planning process. The AAR/IP captures recommendations for post-exercise improvements and defines specific corrective actions.
- **Exercise Evaluation and Improvement Planning Guidance.** HSEEP offers comprehensive guidance on how to evaluate and document exercises, as well as how to implement an Improvement Plan (IP).

These tools will be reviewed in depth later in this course.

Lesson Summary

In this lesson, you learned:

The purpose of the Homeland Security Exercise and Evaluation Program (HSEEP) is to provide a national standard for exercises.

HSEEP is based on capabilities-based planning and emphasizes the need to build capabilities suitable for responding to a wide range of hazards.

The eight steps of the HSEEP exercise evaluation and improvement planning process are:

1. Plan and Organize the Evaluation.
2. Observe the Exercise and Collect Data.
3. Analyze Data.
4. Develop the Draft After-Action Report (AAR).
5. Conduct an After-Action Conference.
6. Identify Improvements to be Implemented.
7. Finalize the After-Action Report/Improvement Plan (AAR/IP).
8. Track Implementation.

After the exercise is over, the jurisdiction's program managers track the implementation of corrective actions listed in the AAR/IP.

By tracking and recording progress on corrective actions, the jurisdiction engages in a continuous Corrective Action Program (CAP).

HSEEP offers tools and resources to support exercise planners throughout its eight-step process. These tools include:

- Exercise Evaluation Guides (EEGs).
- After-Action Report/Improvement Plan (AAR/IP) Template.
- Exercise Evaluation and Improvement Planning Guidance.

Lesson 3: Planning and Organizing the Evaluation

Lesson Overview

This lesson explains how to plan and organize exercise evaluations.

Lesson Objectives

After completing this lesson, you will be able to:

- Define the pre-exercise responsibilities of the Exercise Planning Team.
- Describe how capabilities and objectives impact evaluation requirements.
- Identify key evaluation tools and documentation.
- List key elements in recruiting, assigning, and training evaluators.
- Identify the contents of the Controller/Evaluator (C/E) briefing.

Planning and Organizing the Evaluation

Planning and organizing the evaluation is the first step of the exercise evaluation and improvement planning process. It is the responsibility of the Exercise Planning Team.

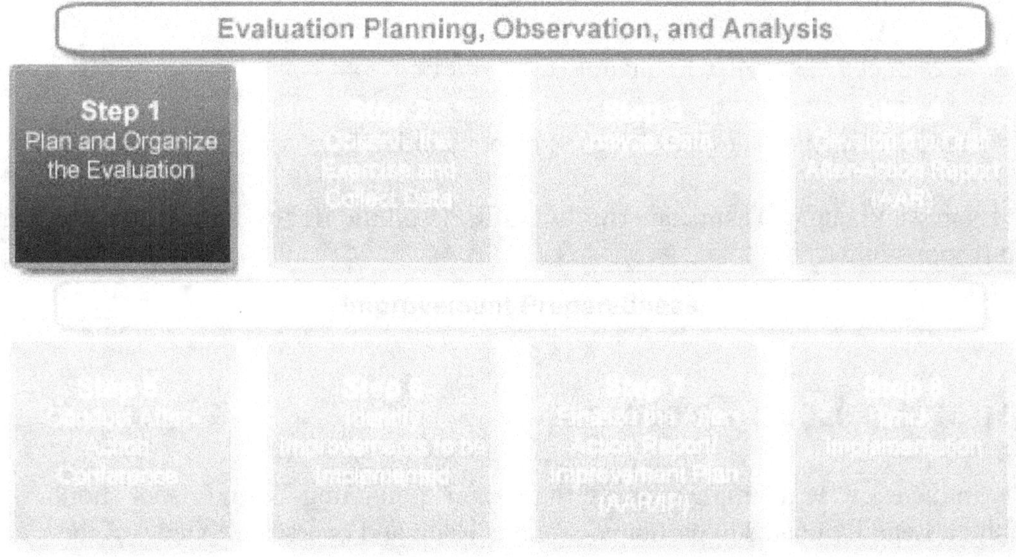

Exercise Planning Team

The Exercise Planning Team structures the exercise and oversees its execution. The Team typically includes members from each major jurisdiction and agency that is participating in the exercise. These members may include:

- Emergency program managers.
- Exercise officers.
- Training officers.
- Department heads.

The members may represent any major discipline in the emergency response community, including law enforcement, emergency medical services (EMS), public health, or fire departments.

One team member will be designated the Exercise Planning Team Leader. This person will oversee the design and development of the exercise, a task which includes managing personnel and delegating tasks.

Exercise Planning Team Responsibilities

To prepare for the exercise evaluation, the Exercise Planning Team will:

1. Appoint a Lead Evaluator.
2. Develop evaluation requirements.
3. Draft evaluation documentation.
4. Recruit, assign, and train evaluators.
5. Finalize an Evaluation Plan.
6. Conduct a Controller/Evaluator (C/E) briefing.

This lesson is structured around these six responsibilities.

The Exercise Planning Team can refer to HSEEP Volume III for detailed guidance on each responsibility.

Appoint a Lead Evaluator

Early in the exercise planning process, the Exercise Planning Team Leader should appoint a Lead Evaluator to participate on the Team and oversee all facets of the evaluation.

The Lead Evaluator should be a senior level individual familiar with the following:

- Prevention, protection, response, and recovery issues and objectives associated with the exercise.
- Plans, policies, and procedures of the exercising jurisdiction.
- Incident Command and decision-making processes of the exercising jurisdiction.
- Inter-agency and/or inter-jurisdictional coordination issues relevant to the exercise.

Appoint a Lead Evaluator

The Lead Evaluator must have the knowledge and analytical skills to undertake a thorough and accurate analysis of all capabilities being tested during the exercise. He or she must also have the management skills to oversee a team of evaluators whose responsibilities vary throughout the exercise.

Before the Exercise

Before the exercise, the Lead Evaluator has four major tasks:

1. Developing evaluation requirements and corresponding documentation, such as Exercise Evaluation Guides (EEGs).
2. Selecting, assigning, and training evaluators.
3. Preparing an Evaluation Plan (EvalPlan), based on guidance from HSEEP Volume III.
4. Assembling evaluator packets that include necessary maps, documents, and an assignment list.

During the Exercise

During the exercise, the Lead Evaluator coordinates the activities of the evaluators. The Lead Evaluator ensures that individual evaluators are:

- In the right locations.
- Equipped with appropriate documentation and supplies.
- Observing and documenting the achievement of exercise objectives.
- Provided with back-up, if necessary.

In addition, the Lead Evaluator is responsible for:

- Overseeing all activities of evaluators.
- Providing input to the Lead Controller.
- Collating incoming data.
- Providing input to the Exercise Planning Team Leader on objective accomplishment.

After the Exercise

After the exercise, the Lead Evaluator:

- Oversees the analysis of data collected from the evaluators.
- Coordinates the involvement of evaluators in post-exercise meetings.
- Coordinates and reviews the preparation of written reports.
- Oversees the development of the After-Action Report (AAR) based on data analysis, text commentary, after-action briefings, and hotwash discussions.
- Guides the development of the Improvement Plan (IP).

Develop Evaluation Requirements

After selecting the Lead Evaluator, the Exercise Planning Team will develop the evaluation requirements for the exercise. These requirements include plans, documentation, and personnel needed to effectively observe, collect data, and analyze information.

The Exercise Planning Team will base evaluation requirements on the specific priority capabilities that the jurisdiction seeks to test through the exercise.

As you learned in Lesson 2, capabilities-based planning is the heart of the exercise evaluation and improvement planning process. The documents driving capabilities-based planning are the Target Capabilities List (TCL) and Universal Task List (UTL).

When the Exercise Planning Team selects capabilities to exercise, it should reference the TCL and UTL to review associated tasks that should be validated during the exercise.

How jurisdictions define priority capabilities

Under the Homeland Security Exercise and Evaluation Program (HSEEP), a jurisdiction establishes a Multi-Year Training and Exercise Plan to structure its exercise program. The Plan outlines the jurisdiction's preparedness goals and the capabilities associated with these goals.

Exercises are designed to measure and validate performance of these capabilities.

For this reason, the Exercise Planning Team should reference the Multi-Year Training and Exercise Plan when determining which capabilities to validate through the exercise.

Learn more about the TCL

The TCL provides guidance on the 37 capabilities that Federal, State, tribal, and local entities are expected to develop and maintain.

Example capabilities include Emergency Public Information and Warning, Critical Infrastructure Protection, and Medical Surge.

By maintaining these capabilities, governmental entities can prevent, protect against, respond to, and recover from catastrophic events, in order to maintain the level of preparedness established in the National Preparedness Goal.

Responsibility for capabilities is based on the size of the jurisdiction: larger jurisdictions are required to possess all TCL capabilities, while smaller jurisdictions are required to possess only select capabilities.

Each Exercise Evaluation Guide (EEG) corresponds to one capability in the TCL.

Please Note: The TCL is considered a "living" document, and will continue to be refined over time.

Learn more about the UTL

The UTL is a comprehensive menu of tasks that must be performed by governmental and private responders to prevent and respond to a range of threats.

No single jurisdiction is expected to be able to perform all UTL tasks. Instead, governmental entities should choose tasks based on specific roles, missions, and functions.

Entities at all levels of government should use the UTL as a reference in the development of exercises.

Please Note: The UTL is considered a "living" document, and will continue to be refined over time.

After determining the capabilities that the exercise seeks to test, the Exercise Planning Team will use these capabilities to formulate exercise objectives.

Please Note: Exercise Evaluation Guides (EEGs) correspond to capabilities in the Target Capabilities List (TCL). By basing objectives on capabilities, the Exercise Planning Team ensures that objectives are linked to EEGs. In fact, EEGs may be a useful tool in helping the Exercise Planning Team define exercise objectives.

Exercise Objective Criteria

Well-defined objectives provide a framework for scenario development, inform exercise evaluation criteria, synchronize efforts towards common goals, and focus support on exercise priorities.

All objectives should be **S**imple, **M**easureable, **A**chievable, **R**ealistic, and **T**ask-Oriented (SMART).

Simple. Objectives should be straightforward and easy to read.

Measurable. Objectives should be specific and observable.

Achievable. Players must reasonably be able to accomplish all objectives within the constraints of the exercise.

Realistic. Objectives should reflect actual goals of the community in terms of time, resources, and personnel.

Task-Oriented. Objectives should focus on specific operations, not wide-ranging or multi-part missions.

Please Note: Exercise planners should limit the number of exercise objectives to enable timely execution and to facilitate design of a realistic scenario.

Examples of objectives:

Objective: Demonstrate the capability of the Incident Management Team to provide emergency notifications containing information and instructions to the public.

Objective: Demonstrate the capability of the Hazardous Materials Regional Response Team to promptly implement measures for hazmat containment, recovery, and cleanup.

Objective: Demonstrate the capability of the Emergency Operating Center (EOC) Mental Health Coordinator to deploy crisis intervention personnel to the incident site in response to calls into the EOC.

Exercise Evaluation Guides (EEGs)

After identifying the capabilities and objectives that the exercise will validate, the exercise planning team should select corresponding Exercise Evaluation Guides (EEGs).

EEGs are standardized documents designed to provide evaluators with information on what tasks should be accomplished or discussed during an exercise. Each EEG is linked to a target capability from the Target Capabilities List (TCL) and provides standard activities, tasks, and performance measures to be evaluated.

EEGs also include space to record observations and questions to address after the exercise. These questions are the first step in the analysis process and development of the After-Action Report/Improvement Plan (AAR/IP).

The EEGs are not meant to act as report cards. Rather, they are intended to guide an evaluator's observations so that the evaluator focuses on capabilities and tasks relevant to exercise objectives.

Each EEG consists of the following components:

- The EEG.
- The EEG Analysis Sheets.

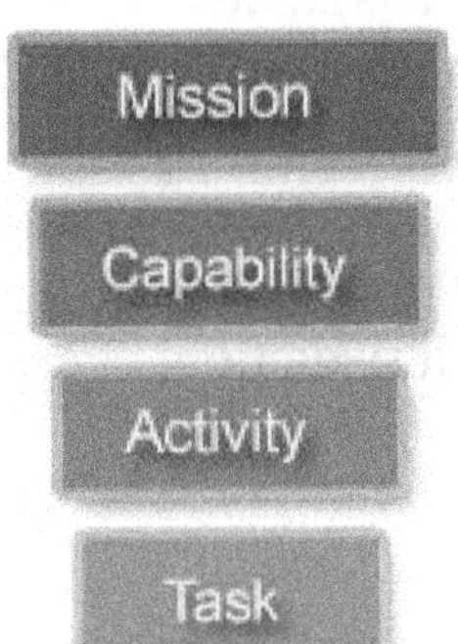

Exercise Evaluation Guides (EEGs) are components of an integrated national preparedness system and process designed to assess a community's preparedness in target capabilities.

The diagram to the right shows the role of EEGs in this system: EEGs guide evaluators in determining whether tasks are accomplished. The accomplishment of tasks determines whether an activity is achieved. The achievement of one or more activities determines whether a capability exists.

After the exercise, deficiencies in key capabilities are captured in the After-Action Reports/Improvement Plans (AAR/IPs). The AAR/IP identifies corrective actions that the jurisdiction will pursue to remedy these deficiencies.

Mission.
The four homeland security missions are Prevention, Protection, Response, and Recovery.

Capability.
Capabilities are specific functionalities that support the high-level mission. They are identified in the Target Capabilities List (TCL).

Activity.
Activities are actions that support a specific capability. They are evaluated by performance measures, which provide quantitative measurements for activities.

Task.
Tasks are specific, discrete actions that support a specific activity. All tasks support the Universal Task List (UTL).

Selecting and Customizing Exercise Evaluation Guides (EEGs)

The Exercise Planning Team will select Exercise Evaluation Guides (EEGs) that correspond to key capabilities under evaluation, based on the exercise objectives. The team may choose to exercise all activities and tasks, or just a select number.

Once selected, the team will customize EEG forms to reflect specific metrics that they want players to achieve. EEGs should be customized to add additional, jurisdiction-specific objectives. They should not be customized to delete or replace pre-existing material.

Please Note: For discussion-based exercises, the Exercise Planning Team should use the performance measures, activities, and tasks for each capability's EEG as questions to drive the exercise discussion. EEGs can also form the basis for customized discussion-based evaluation forms and Situation Manual (SitMan) content.

Draft Evaluation Documentation

As it defines the plans, documentation, and personnel needed for the evaluation, the Exercise Planning Team should keep a record of these requirements. This record is a preliminary template for the Evaluation Plan (EvalPlan).

The EvalPlan is a document that helps exercise evaluators understand their roles and responsibilities. In this way, it supports them to conduct an effective analysis of the exercise and produce a comprehensive After-Action Report/Improvement Plan (AAR/IP).

For discussion-based exercises, a Situation Manual (SitMan) and discussion-based evaluation forms may take the place of a formal EvalPlan.

In operations-based exercises, the EvalPlan is typically part of the Controller/Evaluator Handbook (C/E Handbook).

Recruit, Assign, and Train Evaluators

Once evaluation documents have been drafted, the Lead Evaluator oversees the recruitment, assignment, and training of evaluators.

Evaluators should be non-playing individuals who represent non-participating organizations. (Individuals who represent participating organizations may have biases in favor of their agency.)

The capabilities and objectives tested in the exercise play a critical role in determining how many evaluators must be recruited, their required subject matter expertise, how they will be assigned, and what kind of training they should receive.

Recruiting Evaluators

Evaluators should be recruited for their expertise in a functional area relevant to the exercise. Examples of functional areas include command and control, fire, or law enforcement.

Evaluators should also be recruited for their ability to carry out evaluation responsibilities. Their main responsibilities will include:

- Observing and recording the discussions or actions of players during an exercise.
- Assessing exercise activities against exercise objectives.
- Participating in data analysis and the drafting of the After-Action Report/Improvement Plan (AAR/IP).

Please Note: When developing plans for recruiting evaluators, jurisdictions should consider long-term strategies for developing and maintaining a cadre of trained evaluators.

To fulfill these responsibilities, evaluators should be:

- Experts in the activities they evaluate.
- Familiar with the jurisdiction's plans, policies, procedures, and agreements.
- Familiar with the evaluation system.
- Not burdened with exercise responsibilities other than evaluation.

It is important to recruit evaluators who are able to commit sufficient time to the exercise evaluation.

Please Note: It is helpful to pair a new evaluator with a more experienced evaluator during his or her first exercise evaluation. The experienced evaluator can mentor the new evaluator, improving the quality of the evaluation and increasing the jurisdiction's pool of experienced evaluators.

Assigning Evaluators

Evaluator assignments should be decided upon, recorded, and communicated to evaluators prior to the exercise.

During operations-based exercises, evaluators should be assigned to different exercise play areas on the basis of their subject-matter expertise.

In operations-based exercises, a Master Scenario Events List (MSEL) provides a timeline and location for all expected exercise events. The Lead Evaluator can refer to the MSEL to help determine the times at which specific evaluators should be at certain locations.

Please Note: Evaluators typically do not require copies of the MSEL. In fact, distributing copies may be disadvantageous: if exercise play does not unfold as planned, the MSEL may create confusion and biases on the part of evaluators. A better practice is to provide each evaluator with a schedule of the events occurring in his or her location.

For discussion-based exercises, the assignment of evaluators depends on the number of players, organization of the players and discussion, and the exercise objectives.

Training Evaluators

Evaluator training should occur at least one day prior to the exercise. It should address the following:

- All aspects of the exercise, including exercise goals and objectives.
- Exercise players (group composition and experience).
- Evaluator roles, responsibilities, and assignments.
- How to analyze data.

Evaluator training should also include guidance on observing the exercise discussion or operations, what to look for, what to record, and how to use the Exercise Evaluation Guides (EEGs).

For operations-based exercises, evaluators should be trained according to best practices for observing exercises and recording data. These best practices are described in Lesson 4.

During or prior to the evaluator training, evaluators should be provided with copies of the following materials:

- Exercise documents.
    - For discussion-based exercises, this means the Situation Manual (SitMan).
    - For operations-based exercises, this means the Exercise Plan (ExPlan) and Controller/Evaluator Handbook (C/E Handbook).
- Exercise Evaluation Guides (EEGs) and other evaluation tools and guides.
- The exercise agenda and schedule.
- Evaluator assignments.
- Appropriate jurisdictional plans, policies, procedures, and agreements.

Please Note: The HSEEP ExPlan template and other evaluator resources can be found in HSEEP Volume IV, searchable at https://hseep.dhs.gov/hseep_vols.

Finalize an Evaluation Plan

Once evaluation planning is complete, the Lead Evaluator finalizes the Evaluation Plan (EvalPlan). In less complex discussion-based exercises, the EvalPlan may be communicated orally among evaluators prior to the exercise. For complex exercises, the EvalPlan should be documented and distributed to evaluators.

Whether formally documented or not, the EvalPlan should contain the following components:

Exercise-Specific Information.

The EvalPlan should include exercise-specific information such as the exercise scenario, schedule of events, and evaluation schedule.

Evaluator Team Organization, Assignments, and Location.

The EvalPlan should include a list of evaluator locations, a map of the exercise site(s), and an evaluation team organizational chart.

Evaluator Instructions.

The EvalPlan should include step-by-step instructions for evaluators. These instructions should include what evaluators should do before they arrive (e.g., review exercise materials and wear clothing appropriate to their assignment), as well as how to proceed upon arrival, during the exercise, and following its conclusion.

Evaluation Tools.

The EvalPlan should include evaluation tools such as exercise-specific Exercise Evaluation Guides (EEGs) and blank paper or timeline forms.

Conduct a Controller/Evaluator (C/E) Briefing

Before an exercise begins, the Lead Evaluator should meet with the controllers and/or evaluators to verify roles, responsibilities, and assignments. During this Controller/Evaluator (C/E) briefing, the Lead Evaluator should also provide any significant updates to assignments, the scenario, plans, or procedures.

The C/E briefing is the time for evaluators to ask questions and to ensure that they completely understand their roles and responsibilities.

For operations-based exercises, the C/E briefing often includes a tour of the exercise site so that evaluators know where to position themselves to observe exercise play.

Lesson Summary

In this lesson, you learned:

The key pre-exercise responsibilities of the Exercise Planning Team are as follows:

1. Appointing a Lead Evaluator.
2. Developing evaluation requirements.
3. Drafting evaluation documentation.
4. Recruiting, assigning, and training evaluators.
5. Finalizing an Evaluation Plan.
6. Conducting a Controller/Evaluator (C/E) briefing.

The Exercise Planning Team develops evaluation requirements for the exercise based on the specific priority capabilities that the jurisdiction seeks to test.

Key evaluation documentation includes the Evaluation Plan (EvalPlan), Situation Manual (SitMan), and Controller/Evaluator Handbook (C/E Handbook).

The capabilities and objectives tested in the exercise play a critical role in determining how many evaluators must be recruited, their required subject matter expertise, how they will be assigned, and what kind of training they should receive.

The finalized EvalPlan includes exercise specific information; evaluator team organization, assignments, and location; evaluator instructions; and evaluation tools.

Before an exercise begins, the Lead Evaluator should meet with the controllers and/or evaluators; this Controller/Evaluator (C/E) briefing is a time to provide updates to assignments, the scenario, plans, or procedures.

Lesson 4: Observing the Exercise and Collecting Data

Lesson Overview

This lesson explains how evaluators observe and collect relevant exercise data.

Lesson Objectives

After completing this lesson, you will be able to:

- Distinguish among the three types of reporting.
- Describe the three levels of performance analysis.
- List ways to minimize evaluator effects and errors.
- Distinguish between discussion- and operations-based exercise evaluation.
- Describe the purpose of the player hotwash.

Exercise Observation and Data Collection

Exercise observation and data collection is the second step of the exercise evaluation and improvement planning process.

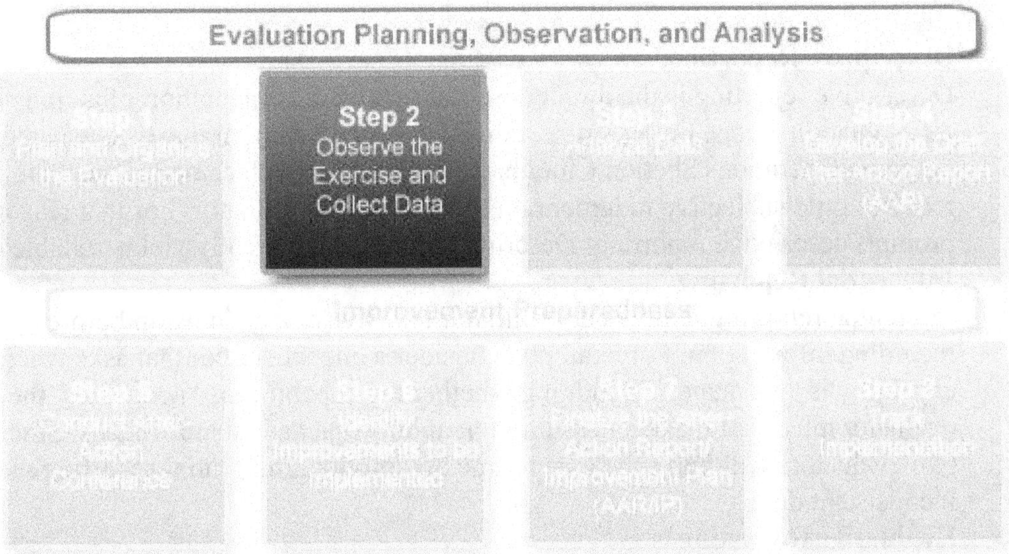

This lesson divides Step 2 into four main topics:

1. The purpose and types of systematic observation.

2. Maximizing the effectiveness of observation.
3. Strategies for exercise evaluation.
4. Organizing data in preparation for analysis.

The Purpose of Systematic Observation

This portion of the lesson addresses the purpose and types of systematic observation.

Systematic observation is the process of using standard forms such as Exercise Evaluation Guides (EEGs) to record performance of critical tasks.

Systematic observation ensures that data is consistent and well-organized. Such data is essential to the development of the After-Action Report/Improvement Plan (AAR/IP), which identifies corrective actions to be implemented and tracked after the exercise.

Tracking progress on corrective actions is the cornerstone of the jurisdiction's Corrective Action Program (CAP). The CAP ensures that exercise findings are translated into concrete action, ensuring continual improvements to preparedness.

Types of Reporting

During an exercise, each evaluator performs three types of reporting:

- **Descriptive Reporting.**
  Descriptive reporting is the direct observation and documentation of actions listed on evaluation forms. For example, consider a checklist item that asks whether the outgoing Operations Section Chief briefed his or her replacement. This item requires little subjective judgment on the part of the evaluator. For that reason, it prompts descriptive reporting. Descriptive reporting typically yields reliable data.
- **Inferential Reporting.**
  Inferential reporting requires an evaluator to arrive at a conclusion before recording information. For example, consider a checklist item that asks whether a capability is "adequate." In judging whether the capability is "adequate," the evaluator must first make an assumption about what "adequate" means. Since no two evaluators will make the exact same assumption, inferential reporting yields inconsistent data.
- **Evaluative Reporting.**
  Evaluative reporting requires evaluators to assess performance on a scale of success. For example, consider an evaluation item that asks evaluators to rate the success of the Incident Commander's communications strategy. This item requires

the evaluator to make an evaluative judgment. Reliable evaluative data is difficult to collect.

For the most part, evaluators will perform descriptive reporting.

Post-exercise activities ask the evaluator to assess data in relationship to exercise objectives. These assessments require inferential and evaluative judgments.

Observing Three Levels of Performance Analysis

During an exercise, evaluators collect data in multiple ways. They record their observations; collect data from records and logs; and attend the player hotwash and the Controller/Evaluator Debrief.

Whatever the data collection method, evaluators should perform three levels of performance analysis.

- **Task-Level Analysis.**

  Task-level analysis focuses on specific, discrete actions. This analysis helps jurisdictions target plans, equipment, and training resources to improve performance on specific tasks.

  Tasks are often linked to performance measures designed to assist evaluators. For example, the "WMD/Hazardous Materials (HazMat) Response and Decontamination" capability contains the task "Implement mass decon operations." This task is accompanied by check boxes marked "Fully," "Partially," "Not," and "Not Applicable."

- **Activity-Level Analysis.**

  Activities are groups of similar tasks that, when carried out according to plans and procedures, support a capability from the Target Capability List/Universal Task List (TCL/UTL).

  For example, the task "Implement mass decon operations" is part of the activity "Decontamination and Clean-Up/Recovery Operations." Other decontamination tasks also fall under this activity.

  Activity-level analysis focuses on whether all activities have been performed successfully and in accordance with plans, policies, procedures, and agreements.

  Through this analysis, evaluators gain valuable insight into broad "themes" of successes or challenges in performing related tasks. Awareness of such themes is key to improving the performance of individual tasks, and thus demonstrating the associated capability.

- **Capability-Level Analysis.**

    Capabilities are specific functionalities that support the high-level mission. They are combinations of elements such as personnel, planning, organization and leadership, equipment and systems, training, exercises, assessments, and corrective actions.

    When conducting capability-level analysis, evaluators examine whether performance on specific tasks and activities was sufficient to demonstrate the desired capability.

    Capability-level analysis is designed to assist managers and executives in developing operating plans and budgets, communicating with political officials, setting long range training and planning goals, and developing inter-agency and inter-jurisdictional agreements.

As you learned in Lesson 3, capabilities, activities, tasks, and performance measures are linked to an overall mission.

There are four homeland security missions: (1) preventing, (2) protecting against, (3) responding to, and (4) recovering from catastrophic events.

Please Note: The After-Action Report/Improvement Plan (AAR/IP) focuses its analysis on activities and capabilities. It includes an analysis of tasks, however, to support root-cause analysis and recommendations for corrective action.

The Value of Coordination in Observation

This portion of the lesson explains techniques to maximize the effectiveness of observation.

In Lesson 3, you learned that training evaluators before the exercise enhances their ability to collect useful data. Coordinating evaluators during the exercise serves the same purpose.

Coordinating evaluators is especially important in large functional or full-scale exercises, when the exercise takes place at multiple locations.

Strong communication is the key to coordinating the efforts of evaluators. During exercises that last two or more shifts, outgoing evaluators should brief incoming evaluators. In addition, evaluators should have a standard procedure for communicating potential challenges to the Lead Evaluator.

Please Note: Coordination procedures should be developed before the exercise. They may be outlined in the Controller/Evaluator Handbook or communicated in the Controller/Evaluator briefing.

Avoiding Common Pitfalls of Evaluation

Evaluations are only effective if evaluators perform systematic observation and generate unbiased records. To ensure unbiased records, evaluators should avoid seven pitfalls of exercise evaluation:

- **Observer Drift.**
  Observer drift occurs when evaluators lose interest or a common frame of reference during an exercise. It is usually the result of fatigue or lack of motivation. Observer drift can be minimized by feedback from the Lead Evaluator, beverages and snacks, breaks, and rotational shifts of exercise observation.
- **Errors of Leniency.**
  Errors of leniency occur when evaluators have a tendency to rate all actions positively. It can be minimized by pre-exercise training.
- **Errors of Central Tendency.**
  Errors of central tendency occur when evaluators describe all activities as average in order to avoid making difficult decisions. It can be minimized by pre-exercise training.
- **Halo Effect.**
  The halo effect occurs when evaluators form a positive impression of a person or group early in the exercise and permit this impression to influence their observations. It can be minimized by pre-exercise training.
- **Hypercritical Effect.**
  The hypercritical effect occurs when evaluators believe it is their job to find something wrong, regardless of the players' performance. It can be minimized by pre-exercise training.
- **Contamination.**
  Contamination occurs when evaluators know how an activity was performed in earlier exercises and permit this knowledge to affect their expectations. It can be minimized by pre-exercise training.
- **Evaluator Bias.**
  Evaluator bias refers to errors that are traceable to characteristics of the evaluator. Evaluator bias can be minimized by careful selection of evaluators, or by employing multiple evaluators to observe the same functions.

Minimizing the Effect of Evaluators on Players

You just learned that data collection can be affected by an evaluator's prejudices. It can also be affected by his or her presence. It is well-documented that when evaluators observe exercises, the behavior of players may change. As a result, evaluators may observe atypical actions.

To reduce this effect, the evaluator should:

- Avoid recording any observations right away, so players become accustomed to the "intrusion."
- Arrive at the appropriate location before players do (this is particularly important if the exercise location is indoors instead of outdoors).

Evaluator presence may also influence players if the players anticipate what evaluators are looking for. For example, players may want to complete a task in a way that is not described in the emergency operations plan, but feel compelled to follow the planned procedure when the evaluator is watching.

Evaluators can minimize this impact by assuring players that the evaluation report will not reflect unfavorably on individuals.

When Evaluators Intervene in the Exercise

You just learned the importance of evaluators keeping a "low profile" during exercises. There are some occasions, however, when evaluators must draw attention to themselves. They may need to intervene to:

- Gather information that is unavailable elsewhere in order to accurately evaluate a capability.
- Clarify a situation that they did not understand.
- Prevent a potentially dangerous situation.

Whether evaluators may intervene during an exercise is decided when the exercise is designed. If evaluators may intervene, they should follow several guidelines:

- **Intervene only when necessary.**

  Remember that the evaluator's presence can distract players. With this in mind, the evaluator should:

  - Minimize questions by jotting them down and waiting to see if they are answered in the course of the exercise.

- o Ask questions at the player's convenience, such as during a lull in exercise play.
  - o Ask essential questions quickly and let players return to their task.
- **Ask questions in language that the player understands.**

If the objective or checklist item uses exercise jargon (for example, "When were players acclimated to the exercise?"), reword the question into simpler terms (for example, "When did the real action begin?")

- **Avoid leading questions.**

A leading question is a question that prompts the responder to think one reply is better than another. For example, imagine that an evaluator is observing an evacuation. Consider the differences between the questions below:

Leading Questions

"Were the citizens evacuated within the appropriate timeframe?"

"Were the citizens evacuated quickly enough?"

Non-Leading Questions

"At what time did you begin evacuating the citizens?"

"At what time was the evacuation complete?"

- **Avoid prompting questions.**

Prompting questions are leading questions that may affect overall exercise play. For example, consider the question, "Have you begun evacuating the affected area yet?" This question may prompt players to act on your suggestion. A more objective question is "Are there any citizens at risk in the affected area?"

- **Avoid the role of advisor.**

Under questioning, players may look to evaluators for guidance. To avoid the role of advisor, evaluators can ask:

- o "What would you do if I were not here?"
- o "What does the plan say?"
- o "What would you do in an actual occurrence?"

Tips for Reducing Evaluator Effects and Errors

In sum, basic guidelines for minimizing evaluator effects and errors include the following:

- Complete evaluator training before each exercise.
- Familiarize yourself with the various types of rating errors.
- Familiarize yourself with the evaluation checklists and report forms.
- If you are missing key data, ask the Lead Evaluator for help.
- Avoid making evaluative and inferential judgments during the exercise.
- Avoid conversations that could influence your impression of the exercise.
- Report obvious evaluator bias - in yourself or others - to the Lead Evaluator.

Use of Exercise Evaluation Guides (EEGs)

This portion of the lesson explains strategies for evaluating the exercise.

As you learned in Lesson 3, Exercise Evaluation Guides (EEGs) identify the activities, tasks, and performance measures that the evaluator should observe during the exercise. Evaluators should complete the EEG so that:

- Events can be reconstructed at a later time (such as during summary sessions).
- Evaluators can conduct root cause analyses of problems.

To ensure EEGs are fully complete, evaluators should:

- Synch their timekeeping with other evaluators before the exercise.
- Record the name and time of the exercise (as applicable).
- Log times accurately.
- Take notes on whether exercise simulations affect the observed task.

Complete EEGs are essential to the development of the After-Action Report/Improvement Plan (AAR/IP).

Discussion-Based Exercise Evaluation

In a discussion-based exercise, evaluators should record discussions as they progress through the exercise. Because existing Exercise Evaluation Guides (EEGs) were developed for operations-based exercises, they should be modified for use in discussion-based exercises.

While recording discussions, evaluators should pay special attention to:

- Issues identified by players.
- How players make decisions.
- Player roles and responsibilities.
- Player coordination and cooperation.
- Recommendations from the group.

Please Note: Both discussion-based and operations-based exercises are followed by a hotwash, but the content of the hotwash depends on the type of exercise. You will learn more about this distinction later in the lesson.

Operations-Based Exercise Evaluation

During an operations-based exercise, the main role of evaluators is to watch and record player actions.

While recording player actions, evaluators should pay special attention to:

- **What** actions took place.
- **Who** performed an action or made a decision.
- **Where** an action or decision took place.
- **When** an action or decision took place.
- **Why** an action was performed or a decision was made.
- **How** players performed an action or made a decision.

Please Note: The evaluator's role is to visually capture the actions of players. Evaluators may need to move around to watch events unfold from start to finish.

Tools for Collecting Data

This portion of the lesson will discuss strategies for organizing data in preparation for data analysis.

Evaluators should select evaluation tools that are appropriate to the exercise's location, size, length, and format. For example, videos, audio recordings, and photographs are particularly useful for gathering information in operations-based exercises. Exercise Evaluation Guides (EEGs) for discussion-based exercises should be customized accordingly.

Immediately after the exercise, evaluators should review their notes for gaps in information. If gaps exist, evaluators can fill them by gathering data from a variety of sources. EEGs are one source. Others include:

- Participant Feedback Forms.
- Event Logs.
- Video or audio recordings.
- Timelines.
- Player notes.
- Incident reports.
- Court recorders.
- Player questionnaires.
- Telephone conversation records.
- Copies of incoming, outgoing, and internal messages.
- Evaluator folders, logs, and timeline.
- Notes from controllers (in operations-based exercises).
- Notes from facilitators (in discussion-based exercises).
- Photographs.

Evaluators may also use lulls in the exercise to begin identifying and filling information gaps.

Player Hotwash

After the exercise, one or more player hotwashes are held. It is attended by the Exercise Planning Team, players, evaluators, and facilitators or controllers. The player hotwash is an opportunity for players to describe their immediate impressions of demonstrated capabilities and the exercise itself. For this reason, it affords a valuable opportunity for evaluators to fill in gaps in their notes.

Player hotwashes allow time for players to address key topics, cross-disciplinary issues, or conflicting recommendations that were identified in earlier discussions. They are also an opportunity for players to comment on how well the exercise was planned and conducted.

Player hotwashes should be held as soon as possible after the exercise is complete, while player observations are still fresh. They are most effective when led by an experienced facilitator who can keep the discussion constructive and focused.

During the hotwash, evaluators, controllers and/or facilitators should distribute Participant Feedback Forms for players to submit.

For evaluators, a hotwash is an opportunity to collect player observations, clarify unclear points, and gather missing information. Although evaluators may be assigned to record a particular group discussion, they should capture information on cross-cutting issues.

A Controller/Evaluator Debrief is typically held after the player hotwash. Attended only by controllers, evaluators, and Exercise Planning Team members, the Controller/Evaluator Debrief is a forum to review and provide feedback on the exercise. It should be a facilitated discussion that allows each person an opportunity to provide an overview of the functional area they observed, and to document both strengths and areas for improvement. Results of the Debrief should be captured for inclusion in the After-Action Report (AAR).

Please Note: The content of the player hotwash depends on whether the exercise is discussion-based or operations-based.

- **Discussion-based.**
  In a discussion-based exercise, the player hotwash is typically held directly after the exercise. Attendees include the exercise players, the Exercise Planning Team, facilitators, and evaluators.

  The goal of this hotwash is to collect player observations on what occurred and why.
- **Operations-based.**
  In an operations-based exercise, the player hotwash is typically held on the last day of the exercise. Attendees include the exercise players, the Exercise Planning Team, controllers, and evaluators.

  The goal of this hotwash is to facilitate players in a self-assessment of the exercise play.

  If a full-scale exercise has several sites, a hotwash should occur at each location.

Preliminary Analysis

After the exercise, each evaluator should gather his or her observations into key issues and a chronological narrative of events. When organized, these observations form the evaluator's preliminary analysis. Preliminary analyses feed the development of the After-Action Report/Improvement Plan (AAR/IP).

At a minimum, an evaluator's preliminary analysis should include:

- A description of the assigned function or operation, analyzed by capability, activity, and critical task, as structured by the Exercise Evaluation Guides (EEGs).
- A documented record of significant evaluated actions (for example, an exercise event timeline).

Lesson Summary

In this lesson you learned:

Members of the Evaluation Team perform three types of reporting:

- Descriptive Reporting.
- Inferential reporting.
- Evaluative reporting.

In an exercise evaluation, evaluators collect data for the three levels of performance analysis:

- Capability-level performance.
- Activity-level performance.
- Task-level performance.

Key pitfalls that evaluators should avoid include:

- Observer drift.
- Errors of leniency.
- Errors of central tendency.
- The halo effect.
- The hypercritical effect.
- Contamination.
- Evaluator bias.

Many of these pitfalls can be mitigated by effective pre-exercise training.

The purpose of the hotwash is to collect player feedback and address key topics, cross-disciplinary issues, or conflicting recommendations that were identified in earlier discussions. While collecting data in a discussion-based exercise, evaluators should pay special attention to:

- Issues identified by players.
- How players make decisions.
- Player roles and responsibilities.
- Player coordination and cooperation.
- Recommendations from the group.

While collecting data in an operations-based exercise, evaluators should pay special attention to what, who, where, when, why, and how actions and decisions took place.

Immediately after the exercise, evaluators should create preliminary analyses of their findings.

Lesson 5: Analyzing Data

Lesson Overview

After exercise play is complete, the job of evaluators is far from over. They are now responsible for analyzing the data collected throughout the exercise, with an eye to improving the jurisdiction's capabilities and capturing lessons learned.

This lesson explains the role of data analysis in a successful evaluation.

Lesson Objectives

After completing this lesson, you will be able to:

- Describe the goal of data analysis.
- Describe the components of the post-exercise Controller/Evaluator Debriefing.
- Identify the four steps of data analysis.
- List methods for identifying problematic issues in the exercise.
- Describe at least one technique for conducting root-cause analysis.
- Explain how to develop effective recommendations for improvement.

Data Analysis in the Exercise Evaluation and Improvement Process

Data analysis is the third step of the Homeland Security Exercise and Evaluation Program (HSEEP) exercise evaluation and improvement planning process.

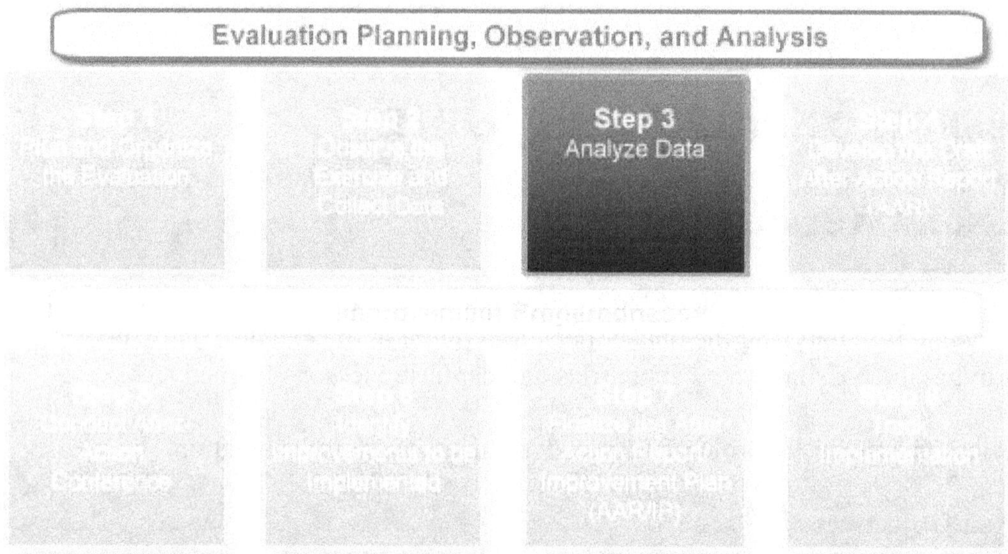

The Goal of Data Analysis

The goal of data analysis is to evaluate the ability of exercised functions to perform target capabilities. For this reason, data analysis may be the most important part of the evaluation.

Reviewing Exercise Objectives

Data analysis is the time when evaluators assess player performance against exercise objectives.

For this reason, evaluators should start by re-reading exercise objectives. These objectives provide the foundation for all data analysis.

If the exercise was complex, evaluators may only need to re-read the objectives related to their assignments.

When reviewing the exercise objectives, consider the following points:

- What was the intent of the objective?
- What would demonstrate the successful performance of the objective?
- If the objective was not met, was it the result of poor exercise design or the decisions of players?

Controller/Evaluator Debriefing

As you learned in Lesson 4, evaluators and controllers meet in the Controller/Evaluator Debriefing after the exercise. This meeting includes controllers because they are frequently teamed with evaluators, and because they can provide insights and observations based on the Master Scenario Event List (MSEL).

The Controller/Evaluator Debriefing allows evaluators to review results of the hotwash and participant feedback forms. It also enables evaluators to:

- **Compare Notes with Other Evaluators and Controllers.**
  The Controller/Evaluator Debriefing enables evaluators to compare notes with other evaluators and controllers. This helps all evaluators fill in information gaps. It also enhances continuity. Consider an evaluator who has notes about a situation that involved follow-up in another situation. If the second situation related to the assigned objectives of another evaluator, the two evaluators must compare notes.

  Comparing notes may also help evaluators resolve discrepancies within their own notes.
- **Refine the Evaluation Documents.**
  The Controller/Evaluator Debriefing enables evaluators to refine their own documentation, if necessary.
- **Develop an Overall Capability Summary.**
  The Controller/Evaluator Debriefing enables evaluators assigned to the same area to develop an overall capability summary. This summary includes associated activity summaries within it.

Please Note: The Controller/Evaluator Debriefing may precede a longer evaluator meeting in which in-depth data analysis occurs. Alternatively, all data analysis may be conducted in one Controller/Evaluator Debriefing. This lesson explains the content of both meetings, although evaluators may choose to combine them.

The Four Steps of Data Analysis

As you just learned, the Controller/Evaluator Debriefing occurs shortly after the exercise. Evaluators typically convene in a more formal meeting later the same week. The purpose of the second meeting, which can last six to eight hours, is to fully analyze exercise data and lay a foundation for the After-Action Report/Improvement Plan (AAR/IP).

In this meeting, evaluators complete four steps of data analysis: identifying issues, determining root causes, developing recommendations for improvement, and identifying lessons learned.

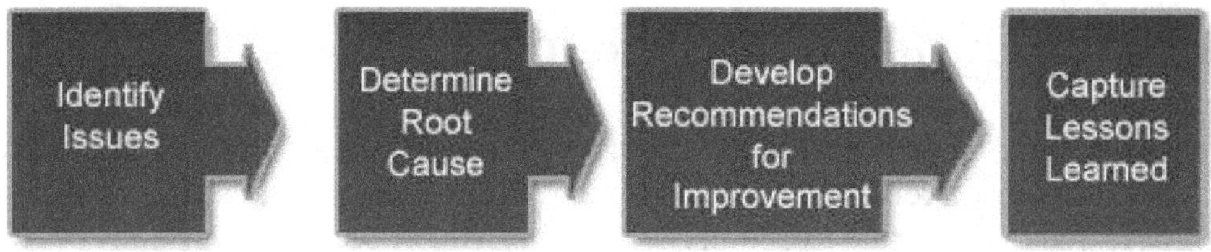

The content of each step depends on whether the exercise is discussion-based or operations-based.

Data Analysis Step 1: Identifying Issues

In both discussion-based and operations-based exercises, evaluators identify issues by comparing exercise objectives to actual performance.

Through this comparison, evaluators identify which capabilities (and their associated activities, performance measures, and tasks) were successfully demonstrated in the exercise. They also identify which capabilities need improvement.

Data Analysis Step 1: Using the Analysis Component of Exercise Evaluation Guides (EEGs) to Identify Issues

Following the Controller/Evaluator Debriefing, evaluators should use the Exercise Evaluation Guide (EEG) Analysis sheets to develop narratives for each capability and associated activity under evaluation.

EEG Analysis sheets have two components:

- **Observations Summary Sheet.**

  The Observations Summary Sheet allows evaluators to record a general chronological narrative of exercise player actions. This narrative is based on the evaluator's observations.

  On the sheet, evaluators should record exercise events, specific actions deserving special recognition, particular challenges or concerns, and areas needing improvement.

  The content recorded on this form will then be used to develop the After-Action Report/Improvement Plan (AAR/IP).

- **Evaluator Observations Section.**

  The Evaluator Observations Section asks evaluators to record and analyze at least three observed strengths and three observed areas for improvement demonstrated by the jurisdiction.

  For each strength and area for improvement, evaluators should record specific observations on what occurred; a root-cause analysis examining why events occurred; and, if necessary, specific recommendations for corrective action.

  The recommendations and observations which evaluators record will be used to develop the jurisdiction's AAR/IP. They will also be the source of proposed corrective actions generated at a post-exercise After-Action Conference.

To complete the Analysis Sheets, evaluators draw data from their Exercise Evaluation Guides (EEGs), as well as from notes, exercise logs, messages, rosters, and other documentation created during the exercise.

Data Analysis Step 1: Identifying Issues in Operations-Based Exercises

During operations-based exercises, evaluators seek to answer the following questions:

- What happened? What did evaluators see?
- What was supposed to happen based on plans and procedures?
- Was there a difference? Why or why not?
- What was the impact? Were the consequences of the action (or inaction or decision) positive, negative, or neutral?
- What should be learned? What are the recommendations for improvements or corrective actions to remedy deficiencies?

Data Analysis Step 1: Reconstructing an Exercise Timeline for Operations-Based Exercises

In operations-based exercises, evaluators reconstruct a timeline of events that occurred during the exercise. (This approach is similar to what most agencies do following an accident or incident.) Evaluators create this timeline using logs, records, and chronological narratives in their own notes.

The reconstructed timeline has three purposes. It helps evaluators:

1. Assess whether actions occurred within the timeframes defined in exercise objectives.
2. Identify discrepancies between what happened and what was supposed to happen in the exercise.
3. Clarify why players made decisions.

The session in which the timeline is reconstructed should be led by an experienced facilitator. To keep the session on track, the facilitator should prioritize areas for discussion.

Data Analysis Step 1: Identifying Issues in Discussion-Based Exercises

In discussion-based exercises, evaluators seek to identify the following issues:

- In an incident, how would response personnel perform the activities and associated tasks?
- What decisions would need to be made, and who would make them?
- Are personnel trained to perform the activities and associated tasks?
- Are other resources needed? If so, how will they be obtained?
- Do plans, policies, and procedures support the performance of the activities and associated tasks? Are players familiar with these documents?
- Do personnel from multiple agencies or jurisdictions need to work together to perform the activities? If so, are agreements or relationships in place to support this?
- What should be learned from this exercise?
- What corrective actions are recommended?

Evaluators gather answers to these questions from their notes and the player hotwash.

Data Analysis Step 2: Determining Root Causes

In both discussion-based and operations-based exercises, evaluators identify discrepancies between what happened and what was supposed to happen. Next, they explore the source of these discrepancies. This second step is called root-cause analysis.

When conducting root-cause analysis, evaluators ask why each event happened or did not happen.

In both discussion-based and operations-based exercises, evaluators identify discrepancies between what happened and what was supposed to happen. Next, they explore the source of these discrepancies. This second step is called root-cause analysis.

When conducting root-cause analysis, evaluators ask why each event happened or did not happen.

A number of analysis tools are available for root-cause analysis. One common tool is the "why staircase."

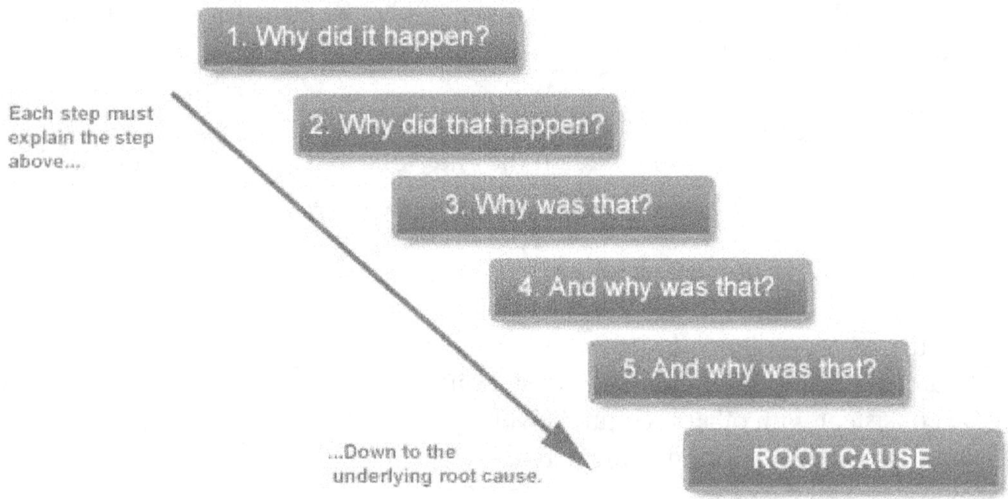

To use the why staircase, evaluators keep asking why an event happened or did not happen until they are satisfied that they have identified the root cause.

When evaluators have identified the root cause of a problem, they can be sure that corrective actions will actually address the problem, and not just a symptom of it.

Identifying the Root Cause

During an exercise, evaluators observed that field teams could not find certain environmental monitoring locations because their maps were different from the one used by the Field Team Coordinator. The evaluators recommended that "all maps used by the Coordinator and the field teams should be the same."

This observation does not address the root cause of why the maps were different. For this reason, it does not ensure that the problem will not be repeated. For example, was the problem a result of how the maps were distributed?

Further discussion revealed that the field teams had actually been given the same map as the Coordinator, but they chose to use the old map because the new map was less clear.

Discovering this, evaluators realized that the recommended solution must also involve improving the new map.

Data Analysis Step 3: Developing Recommendations for Improvement

After identifying issues and their root causes, evaluators develop recommendations for enhancing preparedness. These recommendations will be the basis for corrective actions identified in the After-Action Conference.

Honesty is key when writing recommendations. If you have a criticism, record it. Exercises will only improve preparedness if they are followed by accurate and useful feedback.

Recommendations for improvement should:

- Identify areas to sustain or improve.
- Address both short- and long-term solutions.
- Be consistent with other recommendations.
- Identify references for implementation.

To the extent possible, evaluators should detail how to implement improvements. They can even recommend who will implement them and provide suggested timeframes for completion.

Please Note: Each recommendation should link to analysis and specific observations about an activity. Exercise Evaluation Guides (EEGs) were designed to increase this linkage.

Data Analysis Step 3: Recommendations for Discussion-Based Exercises

When developing recommendations for discussion-based exercises, evaluators should guide their discussion with the following questions:

- What changes need to be made to plans to improve performance?
- What changes need to be made to organizational structures to improve performance?
- What changes need to be made to leadership and management processes to improve performance?

- What training is needed to improve performance?
- What changes to resources are needed to improve performance?
- What practices should be shared with other communities?

Data Analysis Step 3: Recommendations for Operations-Based Exercises

When developing recommendations for operations-based exercises, evaluators should guide their discussion with the following questions:

- What changes need to be made to plans or procedures to improve performance?
- What changes need to be made to organizational structures to improve performance?
- What changes need to be made to leadership and management processes to improve performance?
- What training is needed to improve performance?
- What changes to equipment are needed to improve performance?
- What are lessons learned for approaching a similar problem in the future?

Data Analysis Step 4: Lessons Learned

As the last step in data analysis, evaluators should look for and record "lessons learned." A "lesson learned" is an innovative practice or a piece of knowledge gained from experience. This piece of knowledge provides guidance for approaching a similar problem in the future. Lessons learned allow communities to build on both past experiences and the experiences of one another. For this reason, they save time, conserve money, and accelerate preparedness improvements.

Any lessons learned applicable to other jurisdictions should be included in the After-Action Report/Improvement Plan (AAR/IP).

Please Note: Lessons learned are centralized on the Department of Homeland Security (DHS) Lessons Learned Information Sharing portal (www.LLIS.gov). LLIS allows members of the nationwide response community to learn about, read, submit, and comment on lessons learned.

Lesson Summary

In this lesson you learned:

The primary goal of data analysis is to evaluate the ability of exercised functions to perform target capabilities.

The four steps of data analysis are:

1. Identifying issues.
2. Determining root causes.
3. Developing recommendations for improvement.
4. Capturing lessons learned.

During data analysis, evaluators can identify problematic issues by:

- Comparing exercise objectives to actual events.
- Completing the Analysis sheets of the Exercise Evaluation Guides (EEGs).
- Reconstructing a timeline of exercise events.

Root cause analysis examines the source of discrepancies between what happened and what was supposed to happen. The "why staircase" is one technique for conducting a root-cause analysis.

Evaluators should develop recommendations for improvements wherever they identify that plans, training, or equipment need work. These recommendations form the basis of corrective actions.

Lesson 6: The After-Action Report and After-Action Conference

Lesson Overview

This lesson explains how to develop an After-Action Report/Improvement Plan (AAR/IP), as well as how to conduct an After-Action Conference.

Lesson Objectives

After completing this lesson, you will be able to:

- Describe the purpose of an After-Action Report/Improvement Plan (AAR/IP).
- List the components of an AAR/IP.
- Explain how to write an analysis of a capability.
- Identify the purpose and structure of an After-Action Conference.
- Describe the purpose of the Improvement Plan and the Improvement Plan Matrix.

The Draft After-Action Report/Improvement Plan (AAR/IP)

The development of a draft After-Action Report/Improvement Plan (AAR/IP) is the fourth step of the exercise evaluation and improvement planning process.

The Purpose of Improvement Planning

As you have learned, exercise evaluation assesses a jurisdiction's strengths and areas for improvement in target capabilities.

Improvement planning is the process by which the observations and recommendations recorded in the draft After-Action Report (AAR) are resolved through development of concrete corrective actions. These corrective actions are prioritized, tracked and analyzed by program managers as part of a continuous Corrective Action Program (CAP).

Through this process, evaluation leads to a disciplined process for implementing corrective actions and continually improving preparedness.

The Purpose of the After-Action Report/Improvement Plan (AAR/IP)

All discussion-based and operations-based exercises result in the development of an AAR/IP. The AAR/IP serves multiple purposes. Specifically, it:

- Records what occurred during the exercise.
- Provides feedback on the achievement of capabilities and associated activities.
- Suggests recommendations for improved preparedness.

Perhaps most importantly, the AAR/IP is a tool to establish consensus and buy-in on next steps.

The Homeland Security Exercise and Evaluation Program (HSEEP) has defined a standard format for the development of an AAR/IP.

By using this format, jurisdictions ensure that the style and the level of detail in their AAR/IP is consistent with other jurisdictions. Consistency across jurisdictions allows the nation-wide emergency preparedness community to gain a broad view of capabilities.

Development of the Draft After-Action Report/Improvement Plan (AAR/IP)

As directed by the Lead Evaluator, the Evaluation Team drafts the After-Action Report (AAR) using the evaluative products discussed in Lesson 5. These products include the exercise event timeline, narratives, and Exercise Evaluation Guide (EEG) Analysis sheets.

Other sources of data for the draft After-Action Report/Improvement Plan (AAR/IP) include:

- Data from the hotwash, the Controller/Evaluator Debriefing, and Participant Feedback Forms.
- The plans and procedures of participant organizations.

The plans and procedures of participant organizations are used to compare intended outcomes with actual events.

After-Action Report/Improvement Plan (AAR/IP)

Specifically, the suggested After-Action Report/Improvement Plan (AAR/IP) format includes:

- **Executive Summary.**
  This section is a one- to two-page synopsis highlighting the exercise scope, successes, and areas for improvement.
- **Executive Overview.**
  This section provides background information on the exercise date and time, location, type, hazard, participating organizations, and evaluation methodology.
- **Exercise Goals and Objectives.**
  This section lists the goals and objectives that were identified during the design of the exercise. The goals and objectives are based on the Target Capabilities List (TCL) and Universal Task List (UTL), and should mirror the Exercise Evaluation Guides (EEGs).
- **Analysis of Capabilities Demonstrated.**
  This section provides an analysis of capabilities that were evaluated during the exercise. The analysis should include a detailed assessment of the jurisdiction's ability to perform activities and tasks associated with these capabilities.
- **Conclusion.**
  This section summarizes the key findings of the After-Action Report (AAR) and describes the implication of these findings on future action.
- **Improvement Plan (IP) Matrix.**
  This section should be presented in Appendix A of the After-Action Report (AAR). The Improvement Plan (IP) matrix lists each area for improvement that was identified by evaluators in the AAR. Each area for improvement is accompanied by the following:
    1. Capability
    2. Observation Title
    3. Recommendation
    4. Corrective Action Description
    5. Capability Element
    6. Primary Responsible Agency
    7. Agency Point-of-Contact (POC)
    8. Start Date
    9. Completion Date

Please Note: The details of the IP matrix will be determined by participating jurisdictions or organizations during the After-Action Conference. Although the draft AAR may include suggested improvements, it should not include concrete action items for improvements.

Additional appendices may include lessons learned; a participant feedback summary; an exercise events summary table; performance ratings; and an acronym list.

Writing an Analysis of a Capability

Each analysis of a capability should include the appropriate capability, its title and number from the Target Capabilities List (TCL), and the activities that correspond to it.

Each activity should be followed by:

- **Observations.**
  The observations section should include an overall narrative outlining performance of the activity. It should also include a brief description of specific evaluator observations, which can be positive (a strength) or negative (an area for improvement). If the After-Action Report/Improvement Plan (AAR/IP) includes multiple observations about a single performance measure, it should individually list each observation and the analysis and recommendations associated with it.
- **References.**
  The references section should cite documents that relate to the observation (for example, an Exercise Evaluation Guide (EEG), a plan, a procedure, or a mutual-aid agreement).
- **Analysis.**
  The analysis section should apply root-cause analysis to address whether the jurisdiction possesses the plans, policies, procedures, trained personnel, equipment, mutual-aid agreements, etc., to perform the activity. Where areas for improvement exist, evaluators should list the consequences of action or a lack of action by the jurisdiction.
- **Recommendations.**
  The recommendations section should describe steps that must be taken to address areas for improvement. If the observation is a strength, evaluators can use this section to identify potential best practices and lessons learned.

After-Action Conference Dry Run

Once the draft After-Action Report/Improvement Plan (AAR/IP) is complete, members of the Exercise Planning Team and evaluators meet to review the draft. This meeting is a "dry run" before the full After-Action Conference. Its purpose is to:

- Provide a peer review of the draft AAR/IP.
- Address whether the exercise met its goals and objectives, or whether time constraints or unforeseen circumstances prevented this.
- Review the AAR/IP before it is presented to the full audience.

The outcome of this meeting is the finalized After-Action Conference "read ahead" package. This package should include the draft AAR/IP, conference agenda, and presentation.

The After-Action Conference in the Exercise Evaluation and Improvement Process

Conducting the After-Action Conference is the fifth step of the exercise evaluation and improvement planning process.

The After-Action Conference

Following completion of a draft After-Action Report (AAR), the Exercise Planning Team, Evaluation Team, and other stakeholders meet for an After-Action Conference. The purpose of the After-Action Conference is to review and refine the draft AAR.

As part of the After-Action Conference, attendees develop an Improvement Plan (IP) that articulates specific corrective actions by addressing issues identified in the AAR.

The refined AAR and IP are then finalized as a combined AAR/IP.

Please Note: The Department of Homeland Security (DHS) recommends that exercise managers mark AAR/IP materials *For Official Use Only* (FOUO) and establish a plan to determine the release of these documents to the media or general public.

Structure of the After-Action Conference

Ideally, the After-Action Conference should be scheduled for a full day, within several weeks of the end of the exercise. It should be held at a convenient location or at the site where the exercise took place.

The conference should be highly interactive. Attendees should be invited to validate observations and recommendations, and to provide insight into activities that may have been overlooked or misinterpreted by evaluators.

The conference should include a facilitated discussion of ways in which participating organizations can build upon the strengths identified in the jurisdiction.

Completing the Improvement Plan (IP)

A key purpose of the After-Action Conference is to hold a facilitated discussion on how to implement recommendations for improvement. The outcome of this discussion is a list that identifies corrective actions, the organization responsible for completing them, and a timeline for completion.

When compiled, the corrective actions and timelines make up the Improvement Plan (IP). This IP converts After-Action Report (AAR) recommendations into specific, measurable steps that will result in improved preparedness.

The complete IP is included in the final AAR/IP as a table that summarizes next steps. Participating organizations/agencies will use it to execute improvement planning.

Completing the Improvement Plan Matrix

Conference attendees typically use an Improvement Plan (IP) matrix as a tool to complete the IP. For every improvement recommendation, attendees must complete nine categories on the IP matrix:

1. Capability
2. Observation Title
3. Recommendation
4. Corrective Action Description
5. Capability Element
6. Primary Responsible Agency
7. Agency Point-of-Contact (POC)
8. Start Date
9. Completion Date

Please Note: Recommendations and corrective actions should correspond to those listed in the After-Action Report (AAR). You will learn more about the process of identifying corrective actions in Lesson 7.

The Improvement Plan Matrix and the Improvement Plan

The Improvement Plan (IP) is distinct from the IP matrix. The Improvement Plan (IP) is a narrative that describes changes to be undertaken as a result of lessons learned during the exercise. It describes who will make these changes, as well as the details of their implementation. In contrast, the IP matrix is a tool used to generate the IP narrative, and to gain consensus on improvement actions.

The IP matrix is included in the final AAR/IP as a table that summarizes next steps.

Lesson Summary

In this lesson you learned:

The purpose of an After-Action Report/Improvement Plan (AAR/IP) is to record what occurred during the exercise, provide feedback on the achievement of capability outcomes and associated activities, define corrective actions, and establish consensus and buy-in on next steps.

After-Action Report/Improvement Plans (AAR/IPs) include:

- Executive summary.
- Exercise overview.
- Exercise goals and objectives.
- Analysis of capabilities demonstrated.
- Conclusion.
- Improvement Plan (IP) matrix.

The analysis of capabilities includes a detailed assessment of the jurisdiction's ability to perform activities associated with these capabilities.

When complete, the draft AAR/IP is presented in the After-Action Conference, a forum that allows evaluators to share key findings for feedback and validation.

The After-Action Conference includes a facilitated discussion of how to implement the recommendations for improvement. The outcome of this discussion is an Improvement Plan (IP).

The purpose of the IP is to convert AAR recommendations into specific, measurable corrective actions. By tracking progress of these corrective actions, participating organizations and agencies contribute to a Corrective Action Program (CAP).

Lesson 7: The Corrective Action Program

Lesson Overview

This lesson explains the process of identifying, implementing, and tracking corrective actions in a continual cycle of improvement.

Lesson Objectives

After completing this lesson, you will be able to:

- Describe how participants in the After-Action Conference generate corrective actions.
- Describe guidelines for implementing and tracking corrective actions through a Corrective Action Program (CAP).

Identifying Improvements to be Implemented in the Exercise Evaluation and Improvement Process

Identifying Improvements to be Implemented is the sixth step in the exercise evaluation and improvement planning process.

Generating Corrective Actions

As you learned in Lesson 6, much of the After-Action Conference is devoted to developing the Improvement Plan (IP) matrix. The IP matrix lists corrective actions associated with each recommendation on the After-Action Report/Improvement Plan (AAR/IP).

Each corrective action should identify what will be done to address the recommendation; who (person or agency) should be responsible; and a timeframe for implementation.

A corrective action should contain enough detail to make it useful.

Some After-Action Report/Improvement Plan (AAR/IP) recommendations will lead to clear corrective actions that can be defined at the After-Action Conference. Other corrective actions cannot be identified without additional information. For these items, the IP matrix should specify at least the first step in the process.

Each corrective action should be assigned to the organization that is best qualified to execute it. It is important that organizations are assigned corrective actions that they have the authority to carry out.

Please Note: The IP may be driven by the exercise planners, but it will be carried out by the organizations that participated in the exercise. For that reason, participating organizations must fully support the IP, especially its sections on assigning responsibility and establishing timelines for completion. In short, the development of the IP should be a stakeholder-driven process.

Corrective Actions: Working Within Limited Resources

Some corrective actions will require resources for training, equipment, or personnel. The Improvement Plan (IP) should establish realistic priorities for the use of limited resources. For example, some action items may require steps such as submitting an application for additional funding, or seeking an agreement to share resources with a neighboring jurisdiction.

When resources are not immediately available, exercise planners and evaluators should develop short- and long-term solutions for improving the capability in question. In this situation, the IP is considered complete even if it only details the short-term steps for improvement.

Benchmarking Corrective Actions

Corrective actions must include attainable benchmarks that will allow the jurisdiction to measure progress towards their implementation.

Examples of benchmarks include the following:

- The number of personnel trained in a task.
- The percentage of equipment that is up-to-date.
- The finalization of an interagency agreement within a given amount of time.

These benchmarks should be defined against concrete deadlines so the jurisdiction can track gradual progress toward implementation.

Finalizing the After-Action Report/Improvement Plan (IP)

Finalizing the After-Action Report/Improvement Plan (IP) is the seventh step in the exercise evaluation and improvement planning process.

Finalizing the After-Action Report/Improvement Plan (IP)

After the After-Action Conference, the Exercise Planning and Evaluation Teams finalize the After-Action Report/Improvement Plan (AAR/IP) by incorporating corrections, clarifications, and other participant feedback into the final plan.

The AAR/IP is then distributed to members of the Exercise Planning Team for validation. The Exercise Planning Team will assess whether the AAR/IP is an accurate document that meets the exercise objectives.

When validating the After-Action Report/Improvement Plan (AAR/IP), the Exercise Planning Team ensures that the AAR/IP addresses the needs of participating jurisdictions. It also ensures that AAR/IP is a useful tool to guide the following areas:

- Strategy development.
- Exercise program planning.
- Sharing of lessons learned with homeland security community partners.
- Changes to plans, policies, and procedures.
- Capability development and refinement.
- Efforts to focus limited resources upon improvements in preparedness.

Once the AAR/IP is validated, it is considered final. To protect potentially sensitive information, the Exercise Planning Team should agree on the AAR/IP distribution list before issuing the final version.

Applying Lessons Learned

Among other uses, the finalized AAR/IP serves as a tool to share and apply lessons learned across jurisdictions.

As you learned in Lesson 5, lessons learned are centralized on the Department of Homeland Security (DHS) Lessons Learned Information Sharing portal (www.LLIS.gov). LLIS allows members of the nationwide response community to learn about, read, submit, and comment on lessons learned.

Tracking Implementation

The corrective actions captured in the After-Action Report/Improvement Plan (AAR/IP) should be tracked and continually reported on. This process is referred to as a Corrective Action Program (CAP).

Tracking implementation of corrective actions is the eighth step in the exercise evaluation and improvement planning process.

To track the implementation of corrective actions, each participating jurisdiction should have points-of-contact (POC) responsible for tracking corrective actions and reporting on their progress.

Jurisdictions are not expected to have dedicated staff members for these POC positions. Instead, these duties can be assigned to current homeland security exercise and emergency response personnel.

POC positions include:

- **Event Points-of-Contact.**

  A successful exercise program must have a designated Event Point-of-Contact (POC). This person is responsible for continuously tracking implementation of the corrective actions assigned to the jurisdiction in the After-Action Report/Improvement Plan (AAR/IP).

  The Event POC serves as the central POC for exercise improvements. In this capacity, he or she is responsible for compiling updates on corrective actions into periodic progress reports. In this way, the Event POC executes a Corrective Action Program (CAP).

- **Jurisdiction Points-of-Contact.**

  Each participating jurisdiction should identify a Jurisdiction Point-of-Contact (POC). This person is responsible for managing the corrective actions assigned to the jurisdiction, as well as for assigning action officers to complete individual corrective actions.

  The Jurisdiction POC should collect information from assigned action officers on the progress of corrective actions. After compiling this information, he or she should provide regular progress updates to the Event POC.

- **Action Officers.**

    Action Officers are assigned to complete individual corrective actions. They provide regular status updates to the Jurisdiction POC and/or program manager.

    The Action Officer's reports track progress on the benchmarks associated with each corrective action. These benchmarks were identified in the After-Action Report/Improvement Plan (AAR/IP). Failure to achieve these benchmarks should also be reported, in order to enhance accountability.

    The Action Officers' updates are compiled to produce progress reports on the status of all corrective actions identified in the AAR/IP.

By assigning POCs to track corrective actions, a jurisdiction engages in a Corrective Action Program (CAP) that continually improves priority capabilities.

Continual Improvement and the Corrective Action Program

Exercises are part of a wider preparedness cycle that includes planning, training, equipment purchases, and personnel.

The implementation of corrective actions listed in an After-Action Report/Improvement Plan (AAR/IP) is the way exercises inform and improve other components of the preparedness cycle.

The progress reports issued by a jurisdiction's points-of-contact should illustrate a consistent trend of progress towards the implementation of corrective actions.

Because the AAR/IP ties corrective actions to specific capabilities, progress reports ultimately demonstrate the concrete ways that exercises enhance capabilities.

Once participating jurisdictions have implemented corrective actions, a new cycle of exercise activities can begin.

Lesson Summary

In this lesson you learned:

Participants in the After-Action Conference generate corrective actions. Corrective actions must include attainable benchmarks that will allow the jurisdiction to measure progress towards their implementation.

Examples of benchmarks include the following:

- The number of personnel trained in a task.
- The percentage of equipment that is up-to-date.
- The finalization of an interagency agreement within a given amount of time.

The final After-Action Report/Improvement Plan (AAR/IP) is used for the following:

- Strategy development.
- Exercise program planning.
- Sharing of lessons learned with homeland security community partners.
- Changes to plans, policies, and procedures.
- Capability development and refinement.
- Efforts to focus limited resources upon improvements in preparedness.

The corrective actions captured in the AAR/IP should be tracked and continually reported on. This process is referred to as a Corrective Action Program (CAP).

Each corrective action should be assigned to the organization that is best qualified to execute it. It is important that organizations are assigned corrective actions that they have the authority to carry out.

To track the implementation of corrective actions, each participating jurisdiction should assign points-of-contact (POC).

POC positions include:

- Event Points-of-Contact.
- Jurisdiction Points-of-Contact.
- Action Officers.

Once participating jurisdictions have implemented corrective actions, a new cycle of exercise activities can begin.